DATE DUE

Cities

Claire Llewellyn

Illustrated by
Roger Stewart

Heinemann Interactive Library
Des Plaines, Illinois

Contents

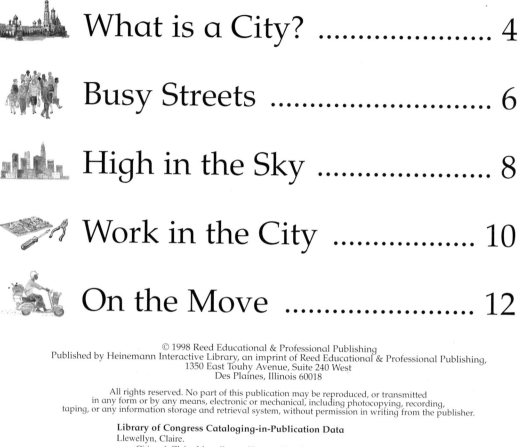
© 1998 Reed Educational & Professional Publishing
Published by Heinemann Interactive Library, an imprint of Reed Educational & Professional Publishing,
1350 East Touhy Avenue, Suite 240 West
Des Plaines, Illinois 60018

Library of Congress Cataloging-in-Publication Data
Llewellyn, Claire.
    Cities / Claire Llewellyn ; illustrated by Roger Stewart.
    p.   cm. — (Inside and out)
Includes bibliographical references and index.
    Summary: Introduces the basic feautres of cities throughout the
world, discussing their streets, buildings, activities, and the work
being done in them.
    ISBN 1-57572-172-4 (lib. bdg.)
    1. Cities and towns—Juvenile literature.   [1. Cities and towns.]
I. Stewart, Roger, ill. II. Title. III. Series.
HT152.L54   1997
307.76—dc21
                                                                97-30493
                                                                CIP
                                                                AC

Acknowledgments
Photo credits: page 5: Tony Stone Worldwide © Paul Chesley; page 6: ZEFA; pages 7, 8 and 15: ZEFA © A. Liesecke;
page 10: Britstock-IFA © M. Gottschalk; page 12: Tony Stone Images © Robin Smith;
page 17: Tony Stone Images © Hiroyuki Matsumoto; page 18: © Pictor International; page 21: Trip © W Jacobs.

Some words are shown in bold, **like this**.
You can find out what they mean by looking in the glossary.

Printed and bound in Italy.
See-through pages printed by SMIC, France.

02 01 00 99 98
10 9 8 7 6 5 4 3 2 1

What is a City?

A city is a place where thousands of people live and work. Like towns, cities have streets, parks, and many kinds of buildings. But cities are large, and some can take hours to cross in a bus or car.

From the air, Paris, France, is a patchwork of tall buildings, busy roads, and green parks. How many bridges can you see on the river?

Many big cities are packed
with people. Some people
live there, but others are
visiting or going to work.

Busy Streets

In the center of the city are banks, offices, and large shops. It's always busy here. Sometimes the streets are jam-packed with crowds of people shopping or rushing to or from work.

Many cities have huge shopping centers with cafés and all kinds of shops.

6

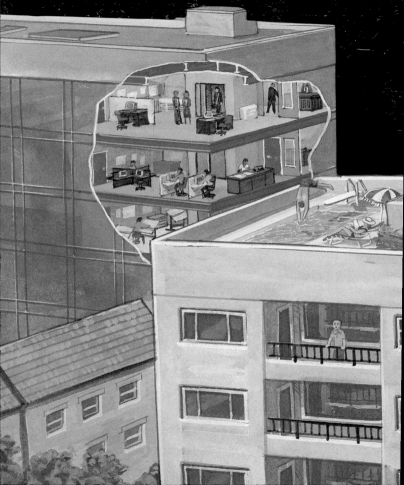

Inside each building, there's
enough room for hundreds
of people to live or work.
There are plenty of stairways,
elevators, toilets,
and phones.

Work in the City

Outside the city center, people work in large factories making cars, computers, and many different kinds of products.

In the factories, skilled workers make the goods quickly and cheaply.

Every city on the coast has a **port,** where the goods are loaded onto ships. Singapore has one of the biggest ports in the world. More than 100 ships dock here every day.

All week, the goods are packed onto trucks and trains and delivered throughout the country. Roads are carefully planned. They carry traffic in and out of the city as quickly as possible.

On the Move

People are always traveling from one part of a city to another. It's easy to jump on a bus or train. Some cities have **subway** trains that make traveling even quicker.

How many different kinds of transportation can you see in this city in India?

Public transportation, such as buses and trains, help keep the city moving. Without it, many cities would be jammed with cars.

12

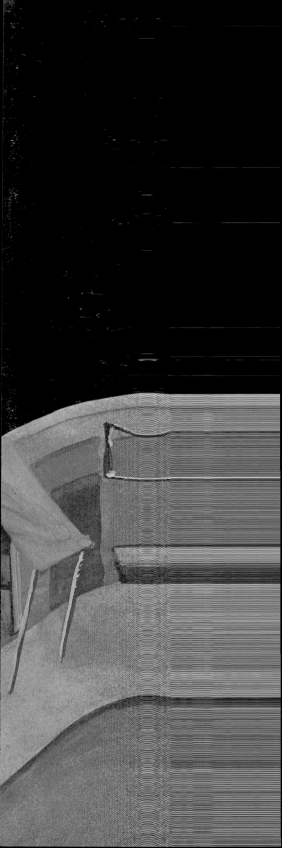

In Sydney, Australia, a **monorail** carries passengers above the streets. It's clean, quiet, and gives a good view.

At Home

There are different kinds of homes in a city. Some people live downtown, near offices and shops. Other people live further out. They have a longer journey home, but their houses are bigger and they have yards, too.

You can find **apartment** buildings in every city. They are a way of squeezing many homes into a very small space.

How many homes can you count in this small section of a city?

Having Fun

There's plenty to see and do in a city. You may be able to visit a zoo, take a tour, or cheer on your team at a sports event.

Some cities are by the sea. Behind the beach is a wide **promenade,** lined with palm trees, cafés, and shops. There may even be a carnival!

Central Park lies in the middle of New York City. This huge green space is the perfect place for a picnic in summer or to ice skate in winter.

Many people visit cities for the museums and **art galleries.** What kind of museum is this?

Celebration!

Every city has special days and events. Crowds gather on the streets to welcome visitors, watch a parade, or celebrate a historical event.

February is carnival time in Rio de Janeiro, Brazil. There are parades, bright costumes, and music!

Bastille Day is an important French holiday. The city of Paris celebrates in style!

Cities in China celebrate their New Year with a dragon dance in the streets. Can you see the legs of the people inside the dragon costume?

Ruined Cities

People have been living and working in cities for thousands of years. Some ancient cities have grown into the huge modern cities of today. Others are empty ruins, where grass grows in between stones.

Athens, Greece, has been a busy city for more than 2,500 years. You can still visit many of its ancient buildings.

The ruined city of Machu Picchu lies high in the mountains of Peru. People left the city when Spanish soldiers invaded it more than 450 years ago.

In some cities, like Mecca, Saudi Arabia, ancient buildings stand next to modern shops and towers.

Famous Cities

Many of the world's cities have become famous for their beauty, history, and buildings that are **landmarks** around the world. Do you recognize any in the pictures?

d.

a.

b.

c.

a. Houses of Parliament, London, England
b. Taj Mahal, Agra, India
c. Leaning Tower, Pisa, Italy
d. The Kremlin, Moscow, Russia
e. The Opera House, Sydney, Australia
f. Statue of Christ, Rio de Janeiro, Brazil
g. Statue of Liberty, New York, USA
h. Eiffel Tower, Paris, France

Glossary

apartment home on one floor of a large building

art galleries public buildings where art is displayed

Bastille Day holiday in France that celebrates freedom

landmark well-known building, monument, or bridge

monorail railway with a single rail

port safe place for ships to dock (sail in and tie up)

promenade walkway along the coast in a city

public transportion way of carrying passengers from one place to another

skyscrapers very tall city buildings

subway electric railroad that runs mostly underground

traditional something handed down from one generation to the next

More Books to Read

Bailey, Donna. *Cities*. Austin, Tex.: Raintree Steck-Vaughn, 1990.

Kalman, Bobbie. *I Live in a City*. New York: Crabtree, 1986.

Steele, Philip. *City Through the Ages*. Mahwah, N.J.: Troll Communications, 1993.

Index